AF615705

Americans All biographies are inspiring life stories about people of all races, creeds, and nationalities who have uniquely contributed to the American way of life. Highlights from each person's story develop his contributions in his special field — whether they be in the arts, industry, human rights, education, science and medicine, or sports.

Specific abilities, character, and accomplishments are emphasized. Often despite great odds, these famous people have attained success in their fields through the good use of ability, determination, and hard work. These fast-moving stories of real people will show the way to better understanding of the ingredients necessary for personal success.

8
BOX NO7
FLORIDA A&M
COACH

Jake Gaither

WINNING COACH

by Wyatt Blassingame

illustrated by Raymond Burns

GARRARD PUBLISHING COMPANY

CHAMPAIGN, ILLINOIS

Picture credits:

Florida Agricultural and Mechanical College: p. 2, 73, 88, 92 94

Alonzo S. "Jake" Gaither: p. 41, 69

Standard Book Number 8116—4552-5

Library of Congress Catalog Card Number: 69-12140

Contents

1. The Stone Face

The boy walked slowly along the railroad track. Sometimes he stopped to pick up a rock and throw it. He didn't try to hit anything. He just threw the rocks to see how far he could throw them, and because he felt good.

It was early morning in October, 1908. The sun shone; the air was cool and clean. Wooded mountains rose on both sides of the track, and high overhead a hawk circled against the blue sky. Watching it, the boy began to sing:

Hawk and the buzzard went to the crow,
Oh, it ain't going to rain no mo, no mo,
It ain't going to rain no mo.

The boy's mother walked ahead of him. Beyond her the tracks disappeared around a curve. And now the boy began to walk faster. He wanted to be close to his mother when they went around the curve. He knew that just around this curve was the great stone face, and the boy was afraid of it. He didn't want to be afraid, but he was. He began to run.

His mother looked down at him and smiled when he caught up with her. She was a small, pretty woman. "It's still a mile and a half to the school. Are you in such a hurry to get there that you have to run?"

"No'm." He was only five—too young to be going to school at all. But his mother was the teacher, and in this small school in the Tennessee mountains, the rules were not very strict.

They were rounding the curve now. Ahead of them was a spot where no trees grew on the mountainside. Instead, there was a great rock cliff. It towered above the tracks, shaped strangely like a man's face—a giant face that seemed to stare angrily down at the boy.

The boy could not take his eyes away from the angry face. He reached up and caught hold of his mother's hand.

"Alonzo Gaither," his mother said, "it seems to me that every day you play along behind me until we come to this place. Then you want to walk so close I trip all over you."

He did not answer. His mother looked down and saw that he was staring at the stone face. "Are you afraid of that, Alonzo?"

"It's—so ugly."

"Yes. But it's interesting too, if you think about how it got there." She explained to him how over thousands of years the wind and rain had beat at the cliff. Soft spots in the rock had worn away. Here and there pieces had crumbled off. "Every cliff and mountain is shaped by nature in this way," she said. "It's just an accident that this one came to look like a face."

"I thought somebody . . ." He stopped because he wasn't quite sure what he thought. "It scares me."

"It's easy to be afraid of things you don't understand," his mother said. "Most folks are. But you must think about the things you learn in school and try to understand them. Then you'll find that a lot of the time being afraid is just foolish."

He wasn't sure what she meant, but he nodded. And they were past the stone face now. Alonzo let go of his mother's hand. He skipped a few steps up the track. He picked up a rock and threw it as far as he could.

2. "An Idle Brain Is the Devil's Workshop"

Alonzo's father was the Reverend J. D. Gaither, a Methodist minister. He was a tall, dignified man with a deep, musical voice. Sometimes when he preached it sounded to Alonzo like big bells ringing. Alonzo was very proud of his father.

The Methodist Church often moved Reverend Gaither from one town to another. Most of them were small mining towns in Tennessee and Kentucky. Sometimes there was no church building. Then

Reverend Gaither would get his people together, and they would build a church themselves.

Reverend Gaither did not make much money. But Mrs. Gaither taught school, so the family always had enough money to get by on.

When Alonzo was thirteen years old, his family moved to Middlesboro, Kentucky. They had been there only a few weeks when Alonzo's father said to him, "I want you to walk downtown with me."

Alex, Alonzo's brother, asked, "May I go too?"

Alex was only eight. His father looked at him and smiled. "All right. I expect Alonzo will have you working for him before long anyway."

"Working for me?" Alonzo said. "What would I have him doing?"

"Come on with me and I'll show you."

They walked into the middle of town. "Look over there," Reverend Gaither said.

Between two stores was a narrow, empty space about six feet wide. "It's summer time, and there's no school to keep you busy," Alonzo's father said. "And an idle brain is the devil's workshop."

Alonzo had heard that saying before. It was one of his father's favorites.

"Yesterday," Reverend Gaither said, "I talked with the man who owns those stores. He agreed to put a roof over that space between them. Then he'll rent the space to you. You'll pay him sixteen dollars a month."

Alonzo stared at his father. He had never had sixteen dollars in his life! "Where do I get the money?" he asked. "And what for?"

SHOES SHINED

"For a shoeshine parlor. You won't have to pay rent the first month. After that, I hope, you'll make the money."

Alex pulled at his father's arm. "May I work there too?"

"If Alonzo wants you. It'll be his business."

His own business! The idea frightened Alonzo, but it also excited him. For the next few days he was busy building shoeshine boxes. He made one for himself and one for Alex. He made chairs out of two large boxes. Carefully he painted a sign: "Shoes Shined." He was so busy he hardly had time to watch the roof being put over his "business."

When the shop was ready, Alonzo placed his chairs against the wall. He put a shoeshine box in front of each chair. He hung the shoeshine sign over the door.

He opened his shop for business early one Saturday morning. A man on the way to work saw the sign. He paused, looked into the shop, then came in. Before Alonzo had finished shining his shoes, another man came in and took the other chair. A third man had to stand up to wait. "You've got a good spot here," the man said. "But you need more help."

"My brother will be here soon," Alonzo said.

When Alex arrived, Alonzo put him right to work. But even with both boys working they had customers waiting. Alonzo's pockets began to grow heavy with nickles and dimes.

It was well after dark when the last customer left. Carefully Alonzo counted his money. He had made exactly nineteen dollars!

At home the family talked about what was to be done with the money. Alonzo wanted a baseball and glove. "That's what you want," his father said. "But the thing you need is an education. You won't have much chance to get ahead in this world without an education."

All his life Alonzo had heard the same thing from both his father and mother. It never occurred to him to doubt them. But he still wanted that baseball and glove.

Suddenly his father smiled at him. "All right, Alonzo. Get the ball and glove. But the rest of the money goes in the bank."

"Yes, sir," Alonzo said.

There wasn't much time to play baseball that summer. Alonzo worked every day in his shoeshine parlor. He was so busy on Saturdays that he had to hire three other boys besides Alex.

Some of the men who came into Alonzo's shop were lawyers. He often heard them talking about their cases. One lawyer might be defending a man accused of murder. Another was trying to convict a woman said to have stolen money. Alonzo listened intently. Sometimes when business was slow, he would run down the street to sit in the courtroom and listen to a real case being tried.

"When I grow up," Alonzo thought, "I'm going to be a lawyer. I'm going to defend people when they are accused of crimes."

3. First Football

Alonzo was sixteen years old when his parents decided he should go away to school. "You'll get a much better education at Knoxville College than you can in Middlesboro," his father said. "And the money you've saved will help meet expenses."

"I'm only in high school," Alonzo said. "I can't go to college."

"The college has a high school too," his mother said. "It's on the same campus. You'll live in the dormitories with the older boys."

Alonzo had never been away from home before. He thought he was going to be homesick and frightened. Later he wrote his mother that there wasn't time to be homesick. He was too busy.

Knoxville College was run by the United Presbyterian Church. All of the students were Negroes, but the teachers were both white and Negro. Discipline was very strict. Students had to go to church and prayer meeting as well as to classes. They had to look after their own rooms in the dormitories. Also, each student had to do some work for the college.

Alonzo's job was to scrub the long hall in the dormitory. He had to scrub it on

hands and knees with water and a brush. Each day the same teacher would inspect his work. If she could find the least speck of dirt, she made him do it over. "Alonzo," she said, "if something is worth doing at all, it is worth doing well. Whatever you do, do it the very best you can."

Alonzo thought she sounded like his mother. A tiny speck of dirt, he thought, wouldn't make the world come to an end. But it was easier to do a good job once than to do a poor job twice. To his surprise, he came to be proud of how clean he could get that hall.

At this time there were no organized athletics at Knoxville College, but the students made up teams of their own. One day Alonzo saw boys in old clothes playing on a field. One of them would grab a strange, oval-shaped ball and run with it. The others would rush at him and knock him to the ground. Then another would get the ball and run.

Alonzo had never seen football before, but he had heard of it. A strange excitement took hold of him. He asked one of the players if he could join the game.

The player grinned at him. "You'd better get two or three years older and about twenty pounds heavier. These other fellows would break you in half."

After that Alonzo stopped to watch the older boys play football whenever he had the chance. Sometimes the ball bounced his way and he caught it. He learned how to pass it back. He learned how to kick. Occasionally the older boys let him practice with them.

Alonzo's roommate was Lewis Carey. He was older than Alonzo. One day he said,

"There's no need for both of us to work every day cleaning up this room. I'll do all the work one day, if you'll do it all the next."

"All right. One day you can be the boss and I'll do the work. Next day it'll be my turn to boss."

From that time on the two boys had great fun bossing one another. Whoever was boss called the other boy Jake. It was "Jake, make my bed. Jake, sweep

the floor. Jake, close the window." Soon all the other students began to call both Lewis and Alonzo "Jake." Alonzo had never liked his real name. Now he was glad to have a nickname.

The year Jake Gaither was a high school junior, Knoxville College hired its first football coach. Now the school could have a real team. There was no rule that said a high school student could not play, so Jake went out for the team. He was six feet tall now and weighed 175 pounds. He did not know much about football, but he tried hard.

"That Jake Gaither," the coach said, "is not as fast as some of the boys, and not as big. But he works hard. He always gives his best, and he's learning."

Before the year was over, Jake was playing end on the varsity team.

One week Reverend Gaither came to Knoxville for a visit. He did not like the idea of his son's playing football. "It's a rough game," he said. "And I don't see that it teaches you anything worthwhile."

Before Alonzo could answer, his father added, "I won't say right now that you have to quit. But I will watch the game this afternoon and decide."

It was a tight game. In the second half the score was still 0—0. Then the Knoxville team had to punt. The safety man on the other team caught the ball and raced back up the field. He broke through the Knoxville line and was in the clear, except for one player. With a flying tackle, Jake brought the runner down.

The tackle knocked the wind out of Jake. He got slowly to his hands and knees as everybody in the stands was

shouting. Then Jake heard one voice he recognized. He looked up.

Reverend Gaither was standing in the bleachers. He had both arms raised above his head. His great musical voice boomed above all the cheering. "My boy!" he shouted. "That's my boy!"

After that Reverend Gaither never said another word against Jake's playing on the football team.

4. The Freshman Reception

After graduating from Knoxville's high school, Jake Gaither became a freshman in the college. He didn't feel like a freshman, for he had been there four years. He had played on the football and baseball teams. He knew his way around. So when he went to the reception given by the college for all freshmen, he was a little bored.

All the teachers stood in line in one big room. The freshmen walked along the line, shaking hands and introducing themselves. Jake went down the reception line, but there was no need to introduce himself. The teachers already knew him.

The line of teachers ended at a door into another big room. Here were bowls of punch and cookies. Here the freshmen stood around talking to one another.

Jake drank a cup of punch and ate some cookies. He was about to leave when he noticed a girl enter the reception room. She was slender and very attractive. As she went along the line, all the teachers had something to say to her.

Watching the girl, Jake moved close to the open door between the two rooms. The last teacher in the reception line stood on the other side, just a foot or

two from Jake's shoulder. When the girl reached this teacher, Jake heard her say, "I'm Sadie Robinson."

"Are you O. T. Robinson's sister?" the teacher asked.

"Yes, sir."

"I knew O. T. when he was here," the teacher said. "He was a very good student. I hope you will do as well."

"Thank you, sir. I'll try."

The girl moved on. She was now directly in front of Jake. Quickly he held out his hand and said in his deepest voice, "You are one of our new freshmen, I suppose."

"Why—yes, sir." She looked surprised. This man did not seem old enough to be a teacher. But he must be, she thought, since he was at the end of the reception line. "My name's Sadie Robinson."

"Are you O. T. Robinson's sister?" Jake didn't wait for an answer. "I knew O. T. when he was here. He was a very good student. I hope you will do as well."

"I'll try." She realized this young man was still holding her hand. She withdrew it and went on to the punch table. When she looked back he had disappeared.

The following day, when Jake entered his Latin class, he saw Sadie Robinson at one of the desks. Quietly he took the seat right behind her. Soon the teacher asked Sadie to translate. When she had finished, Jake leaned forward and whispered in her ear, "You translate Latin very well for a freshman."

She looked around, her eyes wide with surprise. But it wasn't until the teacher called on Jake that she was sure he was a student and not a professor.

When the class was over, Jake walked out of the room beside Sadie. "Don't you speak to me," she said. "I'm mad at you."

Jake began to laugh. And soon Sadie was laughing too.

From that time on, Sadie Robinson was Jake's girl.

5. College Rebel

Jake Gaither was never a real football or baseball star at Knoxville. He was what his coaches called "a good team man." He played to help the team win. Also, he studied football—sometimes much harder than he did his texts. He passed all his subjects, but his grades were only fair.

Jake made his best grades in debating. This activity was even more popular than football at Knoxville College. The school had varsity teams that debated against other schools. Whenever the Knoxville team won a debate, a great bell was rung on campus. Sometimes, when the debate took place at another school, it might be the middle of the night before the other students could be told who had won. Even so, the big bell would boom out. Lights would flash on in the dormitories, and cheering students would lean from their windows.

In his freshman year Jake went out for the debating team. Few freshmen ever made it. But Jake had inherited his father's deep, musical voice. He practiced speaking slowly and distinctly. He understood, too, that in a debate what he said was even more important than how he said it. Often he sat up half the night studying the subject to be debated. And he made the team.

His first debate was held at another school. Few of the students believed that their team, with a freshman on it, could win. But in the middle of the night the big bell on the campus began to ring. The team had won!

By his junior year, Jake was one of the student leaders at Knoxville College. He was on the debating team, the football team, the baseball team. The other students respected him. But Jake was also one of the leaders at getting into trouble. Once a professor refused to allow a group of students to have a picnic. The students did not think the professor's reason was a good one. They appointed Jake to write a protest to the college administration. He wrote such a strong protest that

Young Jake Gaither was a champion debater, an athlete, and a student leader at Knoxville.

the teacher who had stopped the picnic became angry. He wanted Jake expelled from school. But the other teachers did not agree, and Jake remained.

One Sunday afternoon Jake and a group of students started to dance on the auditorium stage. This was strictly against the college rules, and they all knew it. Suddenly one of the teachers came into the auditorium. All the students who had

been dancing on the stage ran out the side doors. But the boy playing the piano did not see the teacher, so he was caught. A few days later he was sent home.

Jake did not believe this was fair. At chapel he stood up and asked permission to speak. It was not just, he said, to expel one student for what fifty or more others had also done.

The president of the college called Jake to his office. Jake admitted he had been one of the students dancing on Sunday. He apologized for breaking the school rules. But he wanted to defend the boy who had been caught.

"In a football game," the president said, "the players must follow the rules. Otherwise it is no real game—only confusion. It is the same with a college. If we did not have rules, there could be no school.

But because you have the courage to tell the truth and to apologize, you won't be sent home."

The trouble that Jake would remember longest began when one of the teachers was fired by the college president. The president was a white man. The teacher was a Negro. Jake and many of the other students believed this was the reason he

had been fired. They began to complain. They staged protest marches and made speeches. They wrote letters to the newspapers.

Again the college president called Jake and other student leaders to his office. The teacher who had been fired was there also.

Carefully the president explained that the teacher's race had nothing to do with his being fired. "Before Mr. Jones was hired," the president said, "he told us that he had done graduate work at a large Northern university. We hired him on this basis. Now we have learned that he did not tell the truth. That is the reason he was fired."

The teacher admitted this was so.

"I did not want to make the matter public," the president said, "because it would hurt both Mr. Jones and the college. But you students have already given part of the story to the newspapers. Now I will have to explain the rest."

Years later Jake Gaither told a friend that he had learned a lesson. "I learned not to go off half-cocked and start a protest before I was sure of my facts. Otherwise, one can sometimes do more harm than good," he said.

6. First Coaching Job

The Reverend Gaither wanted his son to be a minister. Jake was deeply religious, but he was not sure he would make a good minister. He still thought about being a lawyer. But to be either a lawyer or a minister, he would need to go to graduate school.

During Jake's senior year at Knoxville, his father died. Now Jake could not afford graduate school. Instead, he finished at Knoxville and then got a teaching job so he could help his two younger brothers go to college.

Jake taught mathematics, civics, and debating in a Methodist high school in Henderson, North Carolina. He was also coach of all the athletic teams.

The students at Henderson knew very little about organized football. Most of the players just wanted to grab the ball and run. Each one wanted to be a star. Jake taught them to play together as a team. He taught them that every position was equally important. Day after day he drilled them in blocking and tackling.

Some of the players hated drill, and others were slow to learn. Coach Gaither's first team at Henderson did not win a single game. The second year the team did not win, but they played five ties.

During the next six years they lost only six games altogether.

Gaither had been at Henderson only a short time when some of the students came to see him. "Coach," they said, "we want to have a basketball team. Would you coach it?"

Gaither had never even seen a basketball game in his life. He explained this to the boys. "But if you want me to try," he said, "I'll coach the best I can."

Gaither watched some games at nearby schools. He bought a book of rules and studied it, word by word. Then he began to coach.

They did not do well at first. Gaither himself had to learn while he coached. He had to teach his boys to play together, and to understand that it was team play that counted. He taught so well that, in his third year at Henderson, his basketball team won the State Championship.

Sadie Robinson's home was not far from Henderson. During the winters she taught school in Kentucky, but every year she would go home for Christmas. And every Christmas Jake would visit her. Whenever possible, he visited in the summer.

Then one spring Jake got a strange letter. Sadie wrote that everything was over between them. She did not want to see Jake anymore. Someone had told her, she said, that Jake was in love with another girl.

Jake stared at the letter. He didn't know who had told Sadie this story, but it wasn't true. He caught the first train to the town where Sadie was teaching. And before he went back to his own job, everything was all right between them once more. Soon the two were married.

Coach Gaither stayed at Henderson for eight years. His debating teams won several state championships. His athletic teams also won state championships in football, baseball, basketball, and track. They won so many championships that some of the other coaches complained.

Henderson Institute for Negroes was a private school. Several other Negro private schools in North Carolina were turning out good athletic teams. They won most of the state tournaments. This angered some of the coaches in the public schools. They wanted to bar the private schools from state competition.

Coach Gaither knew how much the state tournaments meant to his players. He told a newspaper reporter what the public school coaches were trying to do. This made some of the coaches angrier than ever. They said Gaither had been wrong to talk to the reporter. They voted that the Henderson basketball team could play, but that Gaither could not coach during the tournament.

Before his team left for the tournament, Gaither talked with his players. "Obey your captain just as if he were coach," he told them. "And play your best."

During the tournament the Henderson

team won one game after another. They won the tournament too. The newspapers called them "The Coachless Wonders."

"The Coachless Wonders," one paper wrote, "were the best-coached team in the tournament." Then the paper told how many championships the Henderson teams had won under Coach Jake Gaither.

Soon Gaither began to get letters from other schools. They wanted him to come and coach their teams. So in 1935 Jake Gaither left Henderson and went to coach at St. Paul's Junior College in Virginia.

Gaither had not been at St. Paul's very long before the coaches who had barred him from the North Carolina tournament began to think they had acted unfairly. They took another vote. This time they invited him to come back and be the head referee at their next tournament.

7. End of a Career — Almost

Jake Gaither went to St. Paul's Junior College as assistant coach of football, basketball, and track. After one year he was made head coach.

Gaither knew that he needed more education to get ahead as a college coach. His salary was small. But Mrs. Gaither was also teaching. Together they saved their money carefully. And each summer Gaither managed to go to Ohio State University's summer school.

At Knoxville College Jake had never studied very hard. But he was older now. He understood the importance of learning. At Ohio State he worked hard, and his grades were very good.

One summer Jake and Sadie were living in a rooming house not far from Ohio State University. One of the other roomers was a man named Bill Bell. He was so big that everyone called him Big Bill Bell. Several years before he had been one of the first Negroes to play football at Ohio State. Now he, like Gaither, was doing graduate work. In the winter he was athletic director and head football coach at Florida A&M College.

Big Bill Bell and Jake Gaither became close friends. One day Bell said, "Jake, I need someone at Florida A&M who can be my assistant football coach and also the head basketball coach. Would you like the job?"

"I would love it," Gaither said.

In the summer of 1937 Jake Gaither got his master's degree at Ohio State, and that summer he and Sadie moved to Tallahassee, Florida. There Jake would start his new job.

Gaither told Big Bill Bell about four boys who had played football for him at the junior college. "These are smart boys and good football players," Gaither said. "They ought to have a chance to continue their education. But they are all poor. They can't come here unless they get athletic scholarships."

"All right," Bell said. "We'll get them scholarships."

When the players arrived, the largest boy weighed only 175 pounds. Bell liked

a big team. "Jake," he said, "you ought to be ashamed to have talked me into giving these babies scholarships."

"Wait until you see these 'babies' play," Gaither said.

Bell put the four new boys on the scrub team. In the first scrimmage, playing defense, they drove the varsity back across its own goal in four plays. Bell promptly promoted them to the varsity team.

At this time Florida A&M had only about 800 students. The gymnasium was one barn-like room. The football "stadium" was an open field with a few bleachers. The team had never won a championship of any kind.

The first year Gaither was at A&M, the football team won the conference championship. The next year it won the conference championship and the national

Negro championship. It not only won the championships, but it was not even scored on. And Jesse Mayes, the smallest of the "babies" Gaither had brought from St. Paul's made the All-American team.

Gaither's basketball teams did not do as well as the football teams during his first two years at A&M. But by his third year, the players had learned to work together. They won game after game. "I believe we have a chance to win the conference championship," Gaither told his wife. "But I wish these headaches I've been having would quit."

"You ought to go to the doctor," Sadie said.

"I don't have time now. I'll go when the conference tournament is over."

The tournament was held in Tuskegee, Alabama. Florida A&M won its first

game, then another and another. Finally the championship depended on one last game. Mrs. Gaither went to Tuskegee to watch.

It was a close game. The lead changed back and forth. But Florida A&M won. Sadie Gaither hurried out of the stands to congratulate her husband.

Jake did not seem sure of what had happened. He was holding his head. "It hurts," he said. "I can't think clearly."

Back in Tallahassee the doctor did not know what caused Coach Gaither's trouble. He gave Gaither some medicine and told him to rest.

One day Gaither was driving his car when suddenly he began to see two of everything. His car seemed to have two steering wheels and two engines. There seemed to be two roads in front of him. He didn't know which to drive on.

Gaither stopped his car and tied a handkerchief over one eye. Now he saw only one of everything, and he drove home.

Mrs. Gaither took her husband to the hospital. But still the doctors could not find what was wrong. He kept feeling worse and worse. Finally Sadie telephoned Dr. Earl Odum in Tennessee. He and Jake had played football on the same team at Knoxville. Since then Dr. Odum had become a famous doctor. "I'll be right down to see him," Dr. Odum said.

Dr. Odum examined Gaither carefully. Then he went into the room where Sadie was waiting. "Jake has a brain tumor," he said. "He will have to be operated on right away." The doctor's face was very serious. "Even then, Jake may not live."

Sadie tried hard to keep from crying. At last she asked, "Will you perform the operation?"

"No," Dr. Odum said. "I have a friend in Nashville named Dr. Cobb Pilcher. He is one of the best brain surgeons in the world. I want him to operate."

Gaither was taken to Nashville in an ambulance. There Dr. Pilcher examined him. "I'll operate tomorrow," he said.

Gaither was very weak, but he managed to ask, "How much will the operation cost?"

"For this operation I usually charge a thousand dollars."

"But I don't have a thousand dollars," Gaither said sadly.

The doctor smiled. "Then I'll charge you only one hundred dollars. And you can pay me when you get well."

When Dr. Pilcher operated he found not one brain tumor, but three. Each one contained cancer cells. Now it seemed impossible that Jake Gaither could live. Even if he lived, most people thought, he would never be really well again.

For a long time Gaither was very sick. "But I am going to get well," he told himself over and over. "It's like a football game that I've got to win. I've got to keep trying, keep fighting."

Slowly, little by little, he began to get well again.

8. Head Coach at A&M

For more than a year Jake Gaither was too weak to do any work. But he never gave up; he never stopped trying to get well. Sadie nursed him carefully. She taught English at the college and took care of the household expenses.

While Gaither was slowly recovering, the United States was fighting World War II. Big Bill Bell stopped coaching to join the Navy. After he left A&M, the football teams began to lose more games than they won.

By 1943 Gaither was able to start teaching on a part-time basis. Many people, however, believed he would never again be able to coach football. Dr. Cobb Pilcher had cut away a large piece of Gaither's skull in order to remove the brain tumors. Any hard blow on his head might now be fatal. So Gaither could no longer show players how to block and tackle and run. Even so, he kept thinking about football. He went to the games and saw the mistakes the players made. He kept thinking of new plays and new formations.

In the summer of 1945 the college president came to see Gaither. "With Bill Bell in the Navy, the athletic program here is in poor shape," the president said. "We need somebody to take over as athletic director. Do you think you are well enough to do it?"

"Yes, sir."

"Good. It would help, of course, if you could also coach football. But that is too dangerous. So—"

"I'll coach football," Gaither said, "if I may hire my assistant coaches from among the players who were here when Bell and I were coaching. They know my

Head football coach Gaither and his first Florida A&M coaching staff

way of doing things. They can demonstrate how to make the plays. There will be no need for me to take part in actual contact."

So it was that in the fall of 1945 Jake Gaither took over as head football coach at Florida A&M.

Gaither's players were the same ones who the year before had lost more games than they had won. Now his first job was to make them believe they could win. He remembered what the teacher at Knoxville had told him about scrubbing the hall: *If a thing is worth doing at all, it is worth doing well.* He told this to his players. He told it to them over and over.

"If you are scrubbing a hall," he said, "you must want to scrub it better than anybody else. If you are shining shoes, you must want to shine them better than anybody else. And if you are playing football on this team, you have *got* to play better than anybody else!"

At the same time Gaither taught his players that hard work and doing one's best could be as important as their natural ability.

"No matter how good a player is," Gaither said, "he's got to do his best. Otherwise he's not as good as he could be. And the chances are that he will get worse. But if he does his best, and keeps doing it, he will probably get better. I'm not going to give up on the boy who keeps coming out and giving his best."

Coach Gaither never blamed a player for making an honest mistake. But he did not think that being late for practice or loafing was an honest mistake.

Gaither's practice sessions were run on an exact schedule. From two o'clock to two-thirty one group of boys would work out on the tackling dummy. Another group would work at offensive blocking and still another, at going downfield to cover punts. Each group would have its own assistant coach to help them.

At two-thirty Gaither would blow a whistle. Then the groups of players would change places. But they didn't walk from one spot to another. They ran!

At three o'clock the whistle would blow again. Again the players raced from one place on the field to another. Every man had to know exactly where he was to be at all times.

"A player who won't give his best in practice won't give his best in a game," Gaither said.

Gaither's methods had already made him a successful coach when he introduced his 1967 team to Florida's Governor Kirk.

Many of the players grew tired of the long practices. Some of them might have quit had another coach asked the same amount of work. But Jake Gaither had the strange ability to inspire men. He made them *want* to do their best. Perhaps his training as a debater helped. More likely it was his own deep belief in what he was doing.

"The real purpose of any athletic program," Gaither told his players, "is to build character. And I don't know of any better place to teach men about fair play and hard work than on a football field."

Later one of Gaither's assistant coaches said, "What makes the coach a great man is his ability to communicate with his players. He can make them understand how he wants a play made. He can also make them understand why. And it's not just to win. He can make them want to learn and do their best, win or lose."

Gaither has always been deeply religious. Before his first game as head coach he called his players together in the locker room. "I want to say a prayer before we go out there today," he said.

The boys crowded around him, their heads bowed. The assistant coaches stood

FLORIDA
57
9
65
10
34

quietly in back of them. In his deep, soft voice Gaither prayed not that they would win, but that every boy would do his best. "If we must lose," he prayed, "let us lose with dignity. If we win, let us win with modesty. Amen."

The team ran out onto the field. And they did win. A week later they won their second game, then their third and fourth. Before the season was over, they had won nine straight games and the conference championship.

9. Jake's Boys

Jake and Sadie Gaither have no children of their own. Instead they have "adopted" the football teams that Jake has coached. The Gaithers' pretty brick house within a block or two of the A&M campus is a second home for all his players. Indeed, many of the players think of the Gaithers almost as father and mother. Jake calls them, no matter how big, either "son" or "baby." When he refers to the team as a whole they are "my boys." He treats them with affection, but he can also be stern.

Every scholarship player at A&M has some job to do. One player had the job of sweeping out the athletic department offices. This was supposed to be done early in the morning. But once Gaither found his office had not been swept. He sent for the player.

"Baby," Gaither said, "do you know what time it is?"

The player looked at the clock on the wall. "It's a quarter after nine, Coach."

"Well," Gaither said in his deep voice, "at nine o'clock the President of the United States is in his office working. The president of this university is in his office working. And I'm in my office working." Suddenly his voice boomed like a cannon. "Then why in the world, baby, can't you be working?"

After that the player was always on time.

Because Gaither's players think of him as a father as well as a coach, they come to him with all sorts of problems. Once he was sound asleep when his phone rang. A boy's voice said, "Coach, they've got me in jail for robbery."

The boy was a freshman. He did not even work out with the varsity, and Gaither knew him only slightly. But he got out of bed and went to the police station to find out what had happened.

The boy told Gaither he had been walking across the campus with another student, on his way to a nearby drugstore. The other student had a water pistol that looked like a real gun. With it the football player's friend held up a third student who happened to pass. At this point a police car came by. The police arrested both the football player and his friend who had the water pistol.

Gaither investigated the boy's story and believed he was telling the truth. He had never been in trouble before. Even so, he was sentenced to ten years in jail. Coach Gaither went to see the judge. "If you parole this boy in my custody," he said, "I'll be responsible for him. I'll promise you he won't get into any more trouble."

Finally, the judge agreed.

A few years later this same boy had become a world famous athlete. He won gold medals for the United States in the Olympics. He became a big star in professional football. Yet he was still on parole from prison.

Gaither took the boy to call on the Governor of Florida. He told the Governor the whole story. And soon afterward the boy was given a full pardon.

When it was all over the boy told Gaither, "Coach, there is one thing you won't ever have to worry about again."

"What's that?" Gaither asked.

"You won't ever need to worry about

my getting into any more trouble. Not ever. Because I wouldn't do that to you. If it weren't for your help, I'd probably be spending my life in jail."

Coach Gaither believes that helping his players succeed after college is just as important as helping them win games in college. If he believes that a player has the ability to play professional football, Gaither works hard to get him on a team. He has helped other players get jobs as high school and college coaches.

Gaither got jobs for all four of the "babies" he helped go to A&M his first year in Florida. But when these boys graduated, not one of them had money enough to travel from Florida to his new job. Jake and Sadie loaned them bus fare. Later one of these boys became a successful dentist; another became a well-known

lawyer. One became a captain in the army and then went into government service. The other became a lieutenant colonel in the Army and later, a college professor. Gaither was as proud of them as if they had been his own sons.

Later the college professor said, "Coach Gaither not only helped us get an education and then jobs, but he taught us something more important. He taught us to work and to *want* to get ahead."

Another of Gaither's boys was named Leon Watts. He had been at Florida A&M when Gaither was recovering from his brain operation. Years later Watts himself became seriously ill. He thought he was going to die. Then one day he began to think about Gaither and how he had helped himself to get well after his operation.

Weakly, Leon Watts turned over in bed and reached for the telephone. He called Gaither in Tallahassee and told him about his illness and how he had almost given up hope. Then over the phone he heard Jake Gaither's deep voice saying, "Where's your will to fight, son? Get up. Get up, son, and get well."

Watts lay quietly and listened. And all at once he remembered a football game when the A&M Rattlers had been 20 points behind. At the half Gaither had called his boys around him. "You boys are down now," he had said, "but you can get up. You've got the will to fight. You can do it. So get up and win." And the team did.

Later Watts told a friend, "When I heard my old coach on the phone, it was like hearing that pep talk all over. He made me want to get up and get well. And I did."

10. The "Winningest" Coach

In the years since Jake Gaither took over as head football coach at Florida A&M, his teams have made a habit of winning. In twenty-two years the A&M Rattlers won their conference championship every year except two. They won the National Collegiate Negro Championship five times. They have won a total of 187 games, lost 33 and tied 4. This makes Jake Gaither the "winningest" coach in the history of football.

Through all the years that Gaither has been teaching football to his players, he has been studying it himself. One of the first things he did at A&M was to start a summer clinic where high school coaches could come and study. For teachers, Jake Gaither invited the most successful coaches from big universities all over the country. He not only ran the clinic, he also listened carefully to his visiting teachers. He kept learning.

"Any coach who thinks that he already knows it all," Gaither said, "is not going to be a good coach for very long."

A truly modest man, Gaither tells people that he learns from his own players. One of his favorite stories is about a game he was particularly anxious to win. A&M was behind, and Gaither began to pace excitedly up and down the field. Bob

Hayes, who later became one of the biggest stars in professional football, came up to him. "Coach," Hayes said, "if you lose your cool, how do you expect the rest of us to stay calm?"

Gaither looked at him. "You're right," he said. "Now you go in, Bob, and win the game, and I'll go sit down."

Hayes ran for three touchdowns. A&M won the game. And ever since then Coach Gaither has been telling how he

Gaither with Bob Hayes, who later became a pro football great

was coached by one of his own players.

Honors have poured in upon Coach Gaither. The little city of Middlesboro, Kentucky, where he once shined shoes, has voted him an Outstanding Former Citizen's Award. Knoxville College has given him an honorary degree. The people of Tallahassee, Florida, the home of A&M, have named a park and recreation center for Coach Gaither. In 1961, he was elected to the Helms Athletic Hall of Fame, and in 1962, he was named the National Collegiate Athletic Association Small College Coach of the Year. He was given an award by the Football Writers of America in 1963. In 1964, a new million dollar gymnasium was built at Florida A&M. By act of the State Legislature it was named The "Jake" Gaither Athletic Center and Gymnasium.

As a coach, Gaither teaches his teams sound, fundamental football. But he is a coach with imagination as well. He is always thinking up new plays and new formations. Many of these have been adopted by much bigger and better known universities.

In 1955 Coach Gaither developed a new offensive formation which he called the Split-Line T. During the next seven years his teams, using this formation, averaged over 41 points per game. When they won the National Negro Championship, Gaither was asked to write a book about his formation so other coaches could study it.

The book was called *The Split-Line T Offense*. In it Coach Gaither told how this offense works. But he also told how football can help players to become better and more successful men.

"First of all," Coach Gaither wrote, "football players are students and must be expected to meet the same educational standards as other students . . . Excellence in education is the aim of any good school. The football program must contribute to that goal!"

A player must want to win, Gaither wrote. And he must also be willing to work. "You don't dream the lucky number, pick the lucky horse, or hit the sweepstakes," Gaither wrote. "You have got to work, work, work!"

Gaither also teaches his players that they must get along with other persons. Once the team was playing in the Miami Orange Bowl. Willie Gallimore, an A&M halfback, scored one touchdown after another. By the third quarter he had set a new record for ground gained in a

Coach Jake Gaither with his 1967 coaching staff. He fought illness to become both a great teacher and the "winningest" coach.

single game in this stadium. Then, suddenly, he ran off the field.

"Are you hurt?" Gaither asked Willie anxiously.

Gallimore laughed. "No, sir. But you're always telling us to give the other fellow a chance. We can't lose this game now. So don't you think my substitute ought to get a chance?"

This was typical of the consideration for others that Coach Gaither instills in his players.

After college Willie Gallimore became a professional star with the Chicago Bears. Coach Gaither wrote him a letter. The coach told Gallimore that if he played as well as he could, he would receive a lot of praise. But this praise should not make him conceited. He should keep his head, keep learning, and save his money.

"Do your best at all times to build respect for yourself and your ability," Coach Gaither wrote. "The rest will take care of itself . . . We are proud of you and want you to make good. Just imagine

The game is on! Coach Gaither watches a crucial play from the sidelines.

every time you carry that ball that you are going to get one for the Florida A&M Rattlers."

Gallimore showed the letter to a Chicago newspaperman who wrote a story about it. He wrote that not everyone Gaither coached could be an All-American player like Willie Gallimore. But most of Coach Gaither's boys," the story said, "will be All-American citizens."

Nothing could have pleased Jake Gaither more. All his life he has worked hard to make his boys proud, All-American citizens.